P9-APF-416

Editor: Penny Clarke
Consultant: Stephen Johnson
Page make-up: Mark Whitchurch

Produced by
The SALARIYA BOOK CO. LTD
25 Marlborough Place
Brighton BN1 1UB

© The Salariya Book Co. Ltd MCMXCVII

Published in 1997 by
Franklin Watts
96 Leonard Street
London EC2A 4RH

First American Edition 1998 by
Franklin Watts
A Division of Grolier Publishing
Sherman Turnpike
Danbury, CT 06816

ISBN 0-531-14467-4

Library of Congress Cataloging -in-Publication Data

Martell, Hazel.
  Roman town / written by Hazel-Mary Martell ; illustrated by Mark Bergin ;
created and designed by David Salariya.
    p. cm. --(Metropolis)
  Includes index.
  Summary : Offers a street-by-street tour, not of an actual town but a com-
posite which includes many elements typical of Roman towns throughout
the Empire at the beginning of the first century A.D.
  ISBN 0-531-14467-4 (lib.bdg.) 0-531-15345-2 (pbk.)
  1. Rome--Social life and customs--Juvenile literature. 2. City and town life--
Rome--Juvenile literature. [1. Rome--Social life and customs. 2. City and town
life--Rome.] I. Bergin Mark ill. II. Salariya, David. III. Title. IV. Metropolis
(New York, N.Y.)
DG78.M375   1998
937-dc21   97-7072
                                       CIP AC

Printed in Singapore.

ROMAN TOWN

METROPOLIS

ROMAN TOWN

Written by Hazel Mary Martell

Illustrated by Mark Bergin

PROPERTY OF
THE MONTCLAIR COOPERATIVE SCHOOL

Created and designed by David Salariya

W

FRANKLIN WATTS

A Division of Grolier Publishing

NEW YORK • LONDON • HONG KONG • SYDNEY
DANBURY, CONNECTICUT

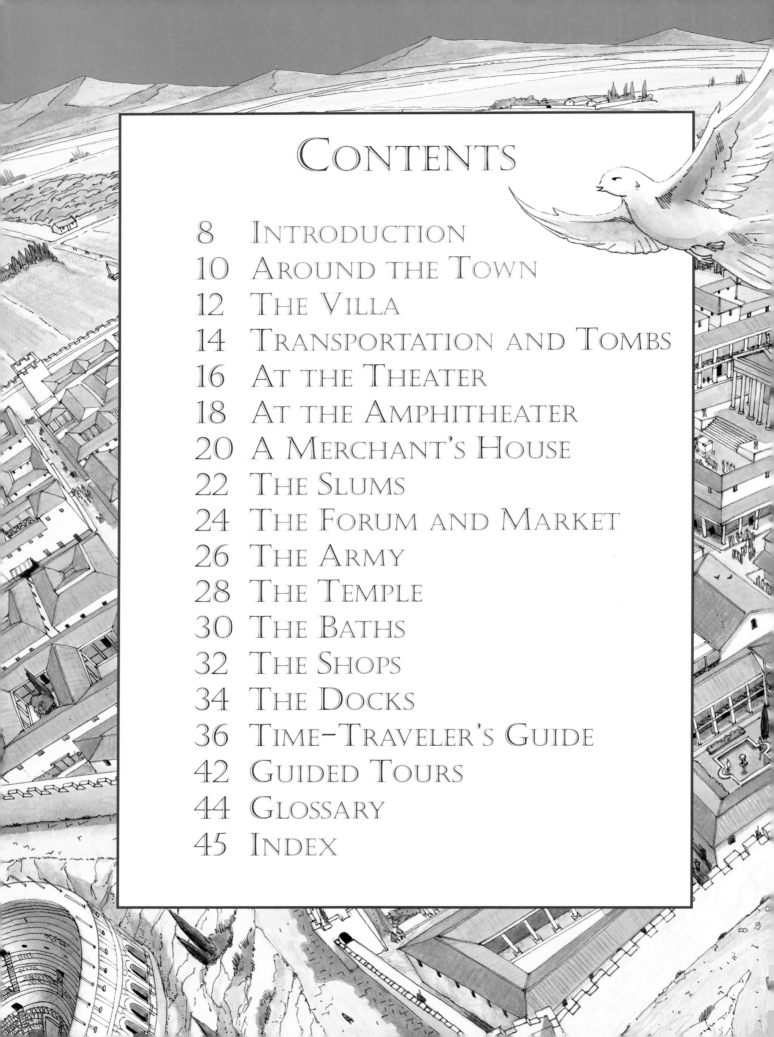

Contents

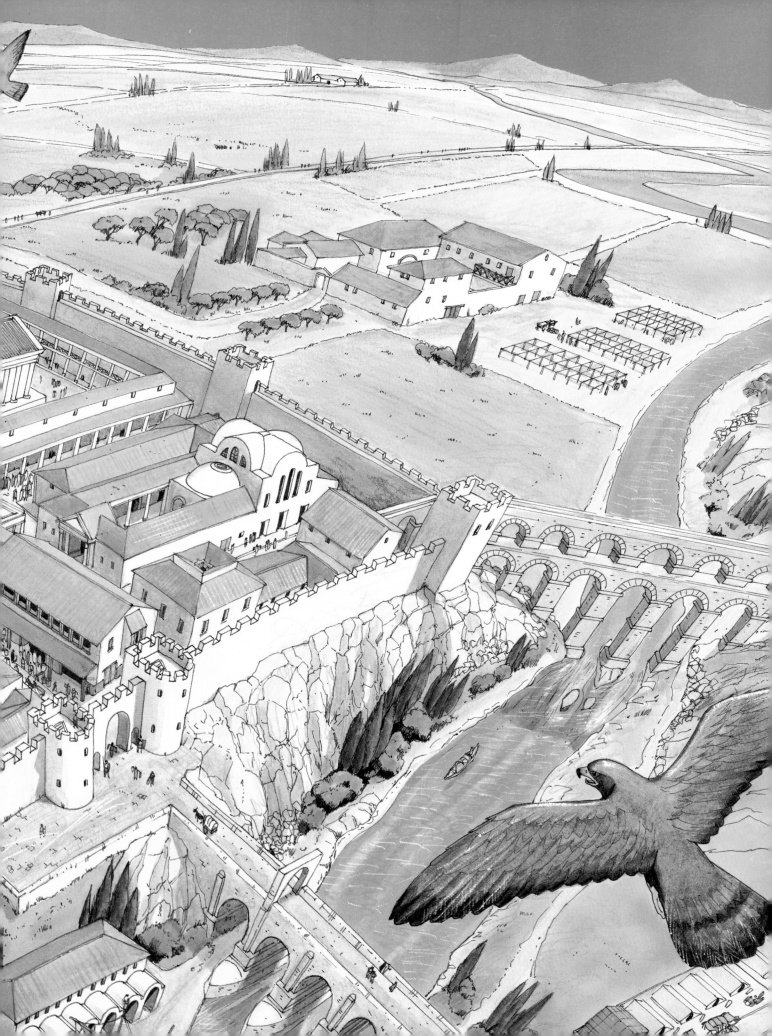

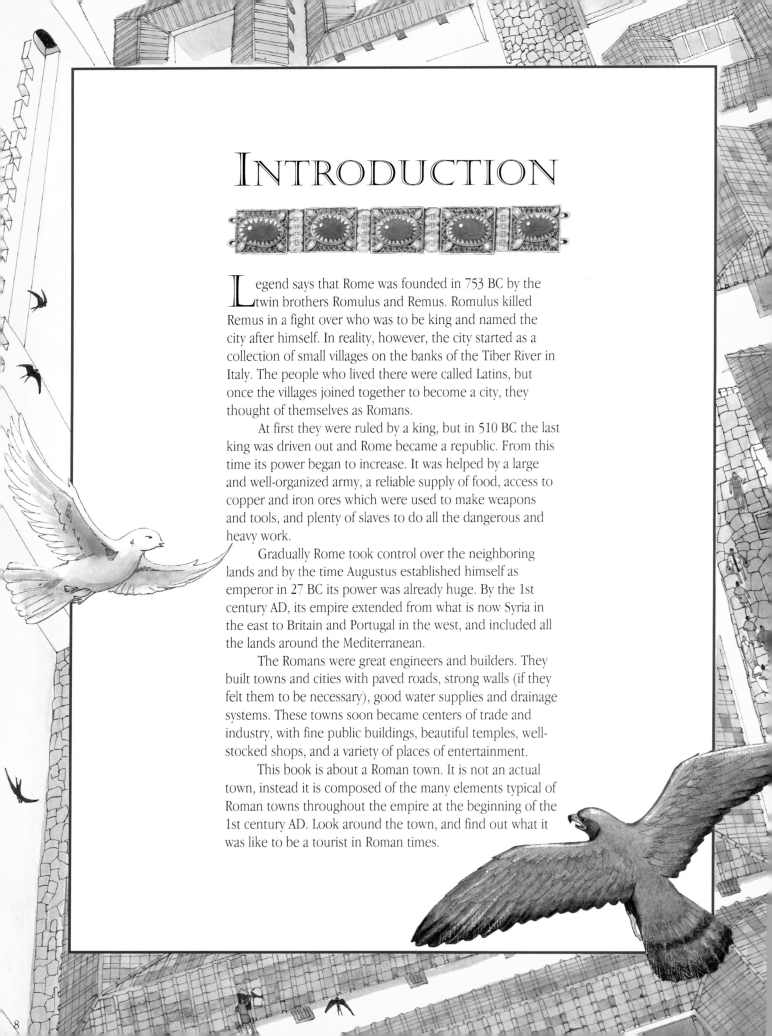

INTRODUCTION

Legend says that Rome was founded in 753 BC by the twin brothers Romulus and Remus. Romulus killed Remus in a fight over who was to be king and named the city after himself. In reality, however, the city started as a collection of small villages on the banks of the Tiber River in Italy. The people who lived there were called Latins, but once the villages joined together to become a city, they thought of themselves as Romans.

At first they were ruled by a king, but in 510 BC the last king was driven out and Rome became a republic. From this time its power began to increase. It was helped by a large and well-organized army, a reliable supply of food, access to copper and iron ores which were used to make weapons and tools, and plenty of slaves to do all the dangerous and heavy work.

Gradually Rome took control over the neighboring lands and by the time Augustus established himself as emperor in 27 BC its power was already huge. By the 1st century AD, its empire extended from what is now Syria in the east to Britain and Portugal in the west, and included all the lands around the Mediterranean.

The Romans were great engineers and builders. They built towns and cities with paved roads, strong walls (if they felt them to be necessary), good water supplies and drainage systems. These towns soon became centers of trade and industry, with fine public buildings, beautiful temples, well-stocked shops, and a variety of places of entertainment.

This book is about a Roman town. It is not an actual town, instead it is composed of the many elements typical of Roman towns throughout the empire at the beginning of the 1st century AD. Look around the town, and find out what it was like to be a tourist in Roman times.

AROUND THE TOWN

A country villa
In the open countryside beyond the town you will find the villa described in detail on pages 12 and 13. It is at the end of a tree-lined road and surrounded by vineyards and fields of crops.

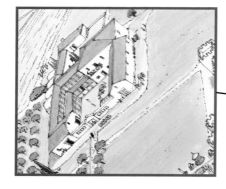

Burying the dead
Tombstones line three of the four roads leading out of the town. You can read more about them and why they are there on pages 14 and 15.

The town's shops
Look on pages 32 and 33 to see some of the things you can buy in this street of shops. They include loaves of bread, jugs of wine, pottery, and jewelery.

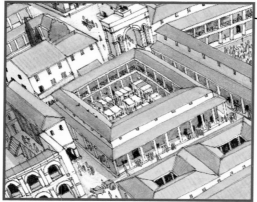

A good day out
The amphitheater is *the* place for an exciting and entertaining day out. You can discover what goes on there on pages 18 and 19.

A luxury home
Wealthy merchants and businessmen live in spacious houses in the town. Some also have a villa in the country or by the sea where they stay in summer to escape the city's heat. This town house is described on pages 20 and 21.

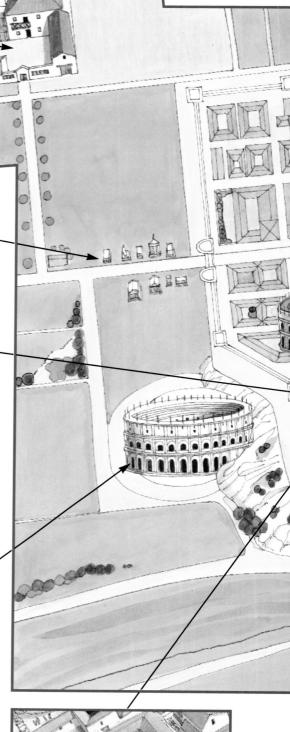

How the poor live
In contrast to the big houses and villas of the rich, poor people have to live in cramped apartments. Find out more about them on pages 22 and 23.

The home of the gods
Temples are the most beautiful buildings in Roman towns. With their graceful columns and elaborate carvings, they are based on designs used by the ancient Greeks. There are more details about temples on pages 28 and 29.

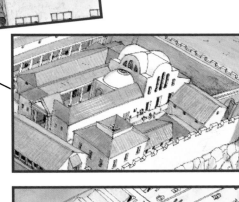

Keeping clean
Only the houses of the very rich have bathrooms of their own, so the public baths are very popular. As you can read on pages 30 and 31, they are a social center, as well as a place to bathe and swim.

The pride of Rome
Part of the army is camping across the river from the town while the soldiers do some training exercises. You can find out how the camp is set up and organized on pages 26 and 27.

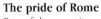

Down at the docks
Warehouses line the quayside of the town's docks. You can read about the town's trade and some of the goods that are stored at the docks, where they came from, and how they were transported on pages 34 and 35.

THE VILLA

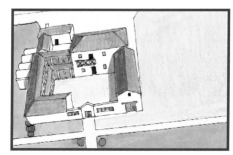

On the outskirts of the town are the villas of the wealthy. Although these luxurious houses are usually at the heart of a working farm, they are well furnished and have fine mosaic floors. The villa has a garden with fountains, statues, trees, flowers, and shrubs. Around the villa are the fields where vegetables and cereal crops are grown. There are also fields for the sheep, cattle, and pigs, which provide meat, milk, skins for leather, and bones and horns for spoons and tool handles.

Work in the house and on the farm is done by the owner's servants, some of whom are slaves.

Olives are crushed in a huge stone press to squeeze out the oil. Then the farm servants sieve the liquid to remove all trace of the olives' skins and stones.

The grapes are put in a vat and the juice squeezed out by slaves treading on them with their bare feet. This is hard work, and the slaves belt their clothes tightly at the waist to stop the sweat running down into the fruit.

This stone carving shows some of the work that takes place during the farming year. Read from left to right at the top and right to left at the bottom. First the fields are plowed. In spring the seed is sown. The ripe crop is cut with sickles (reaping hooks), put on to ox carts and taken to the granary to be threshed (not shown). This separates the grain from the stalks and chaff. Later, the grain will be ground into flour for bread and baked. The man in the middle may be the villa's owner.

Hunting is both a sport and a way of having a more varied diet. Using horses and hounds, or nets, the hunters chase wild boar, deer, hares, and birds.

13

TRANSPORTATION AND TOMBS

The roads leading into a Roman town are usually lined with tombs, and this town is no exception. Most of the tombs date from the 2nd century or later, for that is when it became fashionable to bury the dead instead of cremating them. By law bodies must be buried outside towns. This stops diseases from spreading and saves space in the towns. Most tombs face the road so passers-by can read the inscriptions and remember the people buried there.

There is time to look at the tombs: travel is uncomfortable and slow. Most people walk or use small two-wheeled carts or big coaches.

Government messengers carry official mail on horseback. The good roads make their journeys faster.

Horse-drawn chariot on a coin.

Romans build roads by digging a trench, edging it with curbstones, packing it with layers of stones, gravel, and sand and surfacing it with paving-stones.

At a cremation the funeral pyre is drenched with wine or water. Afterwards the ashes are put in an urn made of glass, marble, or stone.

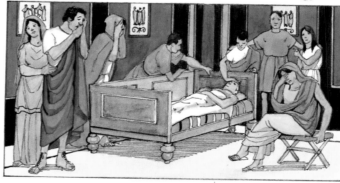

This carving from a tomb shows the funeral procession of the person who is buried in it. There are professional mourners and musicians as well as family and friends.

Few Romans live to be more than fifty and many children die very young. The Romans believe that, after death, a ferry-man takes people across the River Styx to the Underworld, so they put a coin in the dead person's mouth: it is the fare for the ferryman.

Poor people have very simple burials, often just a hole in the ground with no marker or tombstone.

The dead person is carried to his or her grave (or cremation) on an open bier, so everyone can see who has died. Sometimes actors, wearing masks of the dead person's ancestors, take part in the procession.

AT THE THEATER

Roman theaters have tiers of stone seats which are hard and cold, so people take cushions with them to performances to make themselves more comfortable. Each section of the theater has a name and each seat a number. The cheapest seats are at the top, because it is more difficult to see and hear from there than from lower down.

The first Roman playwrights based their plays on Greek dramas, but now the Roman theater has its own styles, including comedies, farce, and pantomime. Two of the most popular playwrights are Plautus and Terence, who write comedies. Audiences will boo and hiss, as well as laugh and clap.

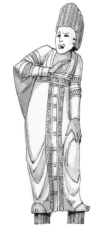

These theater tickets are made of bone. On one side the design relates to the play; on the other is the seat number and part of the theater.

The actors (below) are getting ready for a performance. Two rehearse their lines, while one is helped into his costume and the other chooses a woman's mask for his part. The musician is playing on double pipes, which sound rather like flutes.

To look more impressive and help people in the cheap seats see them better, actors wear platform-soled boots and tall headdresses.

At the ampitheater

Romans go to the amphitheater to watch gladiators fight each other or wild animals, such as lions and bears. Shows usually start in the morning with a procession of gladiators, jugglers, dancers, and musicians. Then there are warm-up fights, often between women or disabled people. These fights are to make people laugh. They are followed by what the audience really wants to see: gladiators fighting each other to the death. After these fights come more mock fights, displays, and perhaps executions of criminals. There is a break for lunch.

The afternoon's entertainment usually consists of wild beast hunts around the arena or fights between wild animals and gladiators.

Different gladiators fight with different weapons. The Romans really enjoy watching unequally armed men fight to the death.

Gladiators with their weapons (top). Spectators decide the fate of a wounded gladiator: thumbs up and he lives, thumbs down and a masked man kills him in the arena.

Armor like this does not always help a gladiator. The bronze helmet (top) protects the wearer's head, face, and shoulders, but restricts his vision. The shoulder-guard (middle) and leg-guard (bottom) are quite heavy, so stop him moving quickly.

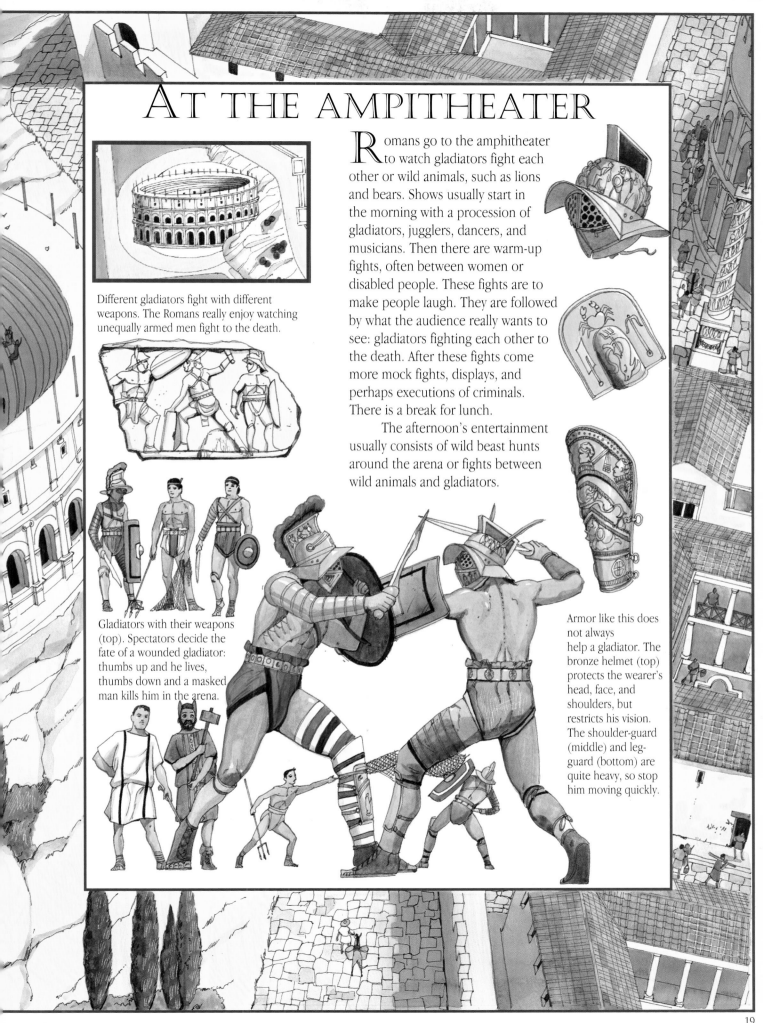

A Merchant's House

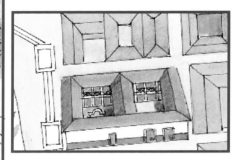

This house, in the middle of the town, belongs to a wealthy merchant. Like the homes of his rivals and colleagues it is built among the shops, but, for peace and privacy, there are no windows in the walls looking on to the street. Instead, all the rooms open on to a central courtyard, which has a fountain, statues, and shrubs. It also has tables and benches, because the family spends a good deal of time outside in fine weather. Water for cooking and washing is piped into the house and drains take the waste away into the town's sewers. Such houses have their own toilets, but everyone, rich and poor, uses the public baths in the town.

At night, the Romans light their homes with lanterns and oil-lamps of bronze or terracotta. In winter, bronze braziers on stands provide extra warmth.

In a wealthy home like this, interior walls may be decorated with stucco, a type of plaster. Skilled craftsmen have molded it into arches and columns, painting them to look like bricks or marble. That view you can see through the window is also just a painting!

Roman furniture is simple in design. Although mostly made of wood, table-legs, and bed-frames are often of bronze and tables for use out of doors have stone or marble tops. At meals, people recline on couches, so dining-tables are always very low.

The house has a large kitchen, because the family entertains a lot. The stove is heated by wood or charcoal.

Mosaic floors are fashionable – and expensive. It takes time and skill to create the elaborate patterns from thousands of pieces of colored stone.

Really large town houses have two courtyards. The first, the atrium, has a small ornamental pool and is used for receiving guests. The second, the impluvium, has a larger pond for collecting rainwater.

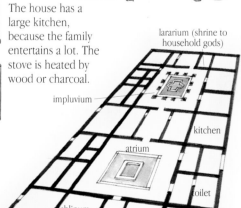

lararium (shrine to household gods)

impluvium

kitchen

atrium

toilet

tablinum (study)

triclinium (dining room)

entrance from street

20

THE SLUMS

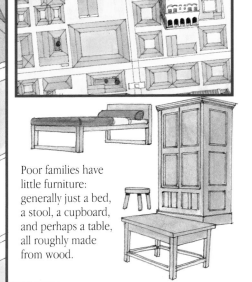

Poor people live in apartment blocks. In Rome these are up to seven stories high, but in a provincial town like this they are only four or five stories. The poorest families generally live on the top floor in the smallest apartments. The lower stories are usually built of stone, while the upper ones are wooden. The ground-floor rooms are shops or taverns. Apartment blocks have no running water. Instead people have to collect their water from the nearby public fountains, then carry the heavy water jars home. There are no drains, so everyone uses the public toilets at street level. Trash is just thrown into the street.

Poor families have little furniture: generally just a bed, a stool, a cupboard, and perhaps a table, all roughly made from wood.

Poor women dress their families as best they can – usually in patched and mended clothes that once belonged to a richer family.

The narrow, crowded streets are full of people buying and selling, jostling with heavily laden carts and with herds of animals being taken to the market.

In summer the smell in the streets is appalling. It comes mainly from the trash and the butchers' shops. But, winter or summer, there's also a strong smell of cooking. Few apartments have kitchens, so people eat in one of the many taverns, or buy cooked food from street stalls.

THE FORUM AND MARKET

The forum is a large courtyard, with a public fountain and a shrine to Ceres, the goddess of the harvest and plenty. People meet here each day to discuss business and local affairs and any news from Rome. Near the forum are shops, offices, and places to eat. The town's most important public buildings are around the edge of the forum. These include the basilica, which serves as the town hall and law courts, the curia where the town council meets, the treasury where the money belonging to the town is kept, and the tabularium where all the official documents, such as tax records, are stored.

The magistrates are escorted by lictors – men who carry an ax in a bundle of rods to symbolize the magistrates' power.

Roman towns are governed by two magistrates. They also act as judges, trying and sentencing criminals.

The forum bustles with life on market days, when traders and farmers set up stalls to sell food and other goods.

Crimes are often punished with a fine. The richer the person, the heavier the fine.

Some criminals are sent to the mines, where many will die from poor food and overwork.

Other punishments include exile to remote parts of the empire, confiscation of property, and loss of citizenship.

Criminals sentenced to death go to the amphitheater. There they fight gladiators or wild animals to entertain the crowds.

THE ARMY

Rome won its vast empire largely through the size and skill of its army. In peacetime the soldiers train by going on very long marches and building camps far from their permanent forts. First they mark out the square campsite, then they dig a ditch around it. Earth from the ditch is made into a mound and a wooden fence is built on top. Leather tents are pitched in lines of ten, with eight men to a tent. At the end of each line is the centurion's tent. As well as practising fighting, the soldiers build bridges, roads, and aqueducts in the towns where they camp.

The Romans are very proud of their army. This carving shows it defeating the Dacians of eastern Europe.

helmet

spear

protective face pieces

metal strips to protect body and shoulders

Legionaries wear metal helmets, jackets of metal strips backed with leather, woolen tunics, leather belts, groin guards, and hobnailed sandals. Each also has a sword, dagger, spear, and shield.

The army's best troops are the legions, each of about 5,000 foot soldiers. Every legion has 10 cohorts subdivided into centuries of 80 men. A century is led by a centurion.

sword

hobnailed sandals

shield

Legionaries have to buy and cook their own food. They eat mostly bread, cheese, lentils, peas, and beans, and drink cheap red wine. When they are on the march, each man carries enough food for three days.

THE TEMPLE

The Romans have many different gods and goddesses. Each family has its own household gods that are worshipped every day at a small shrine in their home. The most important gods have temples in the town. The people believe these are the gods' homes and put statues of the gods in them. Some also have war trophies: chariots and armor from defeated enemies. In front of each large temple is an altar where priests make sacrifices to keep the gods happy or to ask them favors. People bring animals, such as sheep or oxen, to the temple to be killed. A special priest, the haruspex, then examines the intestines of the dead animal to find out if the gods are pleased or angry.

The chief god is Jupiter, god of the sky and thunder. He carries thunderbolts.

Neptune is god of the sea. His symbol is a trident.

Minerva, goddess of wisdom, crafts, and war, carries a spear and shield.

Juno (left), Jupiter's wife and sister, is goddess of women and children. Venus (below) is goddess of love and beauty.

People fear Pluto (left), god of the Underworld.

Vesta (far left) is the goddess of purity, fire, and the hearth. A sacred flame burns in her temple in Rome. It is guarded by her priestesses, the Vestal Virgins, and never allowed to go out.

Mars, god of war, is always dressed as a Roman soldier. The month of March is named after him. He is the son of Juno.

THE BATHS

ost Roman towns have at least one public bathhouse where people go to wash, to swim in the various pools, and meet their friends. They leave their clothes with an attendant and go to the tepidarium, a warm room with a small pool. From there they go to the caldarium, which is hot and sweaty, or the laconicum which is the hottest of all. After that it is a relief to have a cold plunge in the frigidarium before a relaxing massage with scented oils. The baths are the town's social center, where people meet and gossip, play games, or exercise in the exercise yard. Some baths have libraries and reading rooms, and gardens to stroll in, while others put on concerts and poetry readings.

Women and girls have a separate bathhouse and changing rooms. They do not use the exercise yard. Well-to-do Romans think it is quite improper for the women in their families to take strenuous exercise. Instead, the mothers, wives and daughters of rich merchants, officials, and politicians will spend time at the hairdresser or beautician.

Rich people take their slaves with them to the baths to help them to dress and undress.

Instead of soap, the Romans rub oil into their skin, then scrape it and the dirt off with a special flat blade called a strigil.

Businessmen go to the baths in the afternoon, when it is too hot to work. If they do not feel like taking any exercise, they sit and gossip, or discuss business while having a drink or something to eat. Then, when the day begins to cool down, they go back to work.

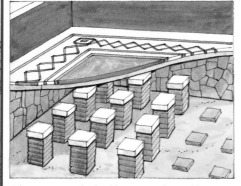

The rooms in the bathhouse are heated by means of a hypocaust. This is a heating system in which hot air from a wood-fired furnace circulates under the floor (which is supported on brick pillars) then up through vents in the walls of the rooms above.

You will have seen items like these on the right for sale in the shops. If you are not sure how to use them, watch the local citizens when you visit the baths. If you do not have a slave to oil and scrape you with a strigil, you can pay one of the attendants at the baths to do it for you. Or go with a friend and take turns to scrape each other down.

jar of oil

pan for pouring cold water over yourself

scraper for removing ear wax

scoop

jar for oil

tweezers

strigil

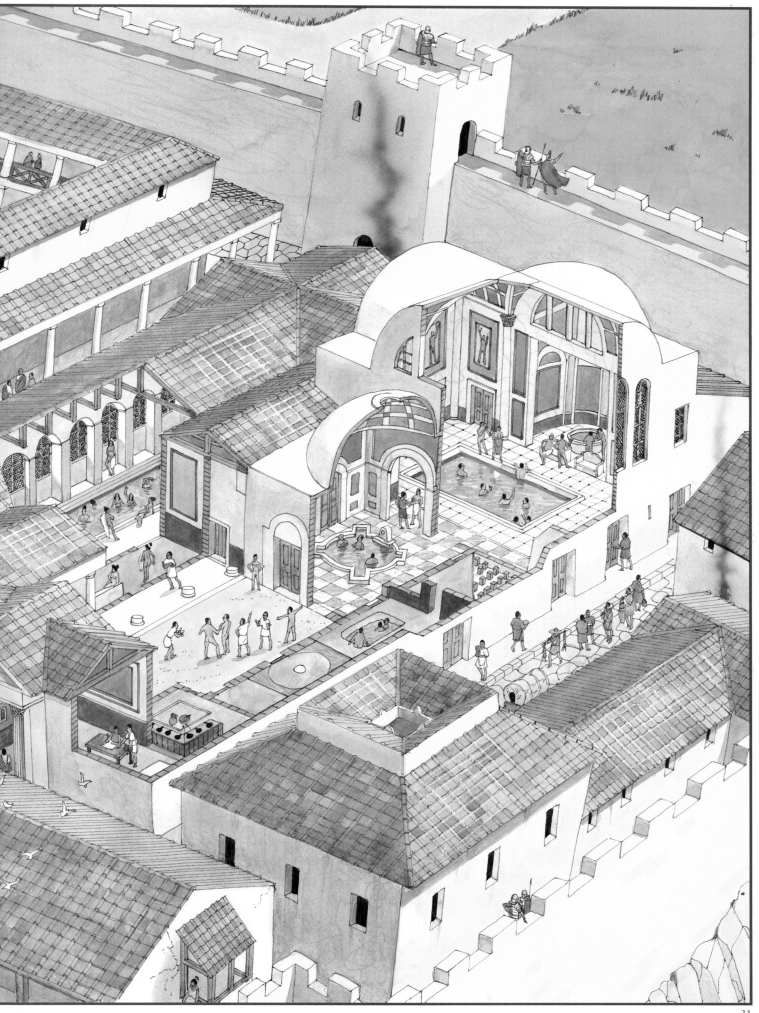

THE SHOPS

The town has many small shops. Butchers, bakers, and pieshops are always busy. Wine and olive oil are sold by the amphora or the jug. Most people take a jug with them to the shop and have the oil or wine measured into it. Amphorae are big and many townspeople have nowhere to store them – even if they can afford to buy such a large quantity of oil or wine. Many shops have workshops at the back, where the goods for sale are made: leather belts and purses, mirrors of polished silver or bronze, bone-handled knives, bone hairpins, gold and silver cups, razors, spoons and kitchenware. Fruit and vegetables are sold at market stalls.

Potters make bowls, jugs, dishes, cups, and cooking pots for everyday use, as well as storage jars in a wide range of sizes.

Bone is used to make combs, dice, and counters for games (above). Glass flasks and beakers (below) are made by blowing a bubble of glass into a mold.

At the shoemaker customers can buy a pair of ready-made shoes or have a pair made to measure. Sandals are always popular, but boots and shoes are much in demand in colder parts of the empire.

Very few people can afford a vase like this – and not many craftsmen can make them. A layer of white glass is poured over a base of blue glass and then cut away to leave the design in white raised against the blue background.

Carving of a goldsmith at work. Above him are his scales (in real life they are not so large) and in front of his workbench is a pile of gold ingots. Among the most skilled of craftsmen, goldsmiths make beautiful jewelery, such as the filigree bracelet below.

AVRIFEX·BRATTI·R

Cloth merchants sell linen and woolen cloth imported from all parts of the empire. Sometimes they even have silk from China.

THE DOCKS

The docks are always a busy part of the town. Wooden sailing ships with goods from all parts of the empire are unloaded at the quayside. The goods are checked by the merchants who imported them before being taken into storage for later sale in the town's shops. Among the goods are wine, pottery, olive oil, and liquamen, a strong but popular fish sauce. Luxury goods for the rich include fine woolen cloth from Britain and silk from China. Goods made of ivory and cups and plates of silver and gold are also imported, but they are too expensive for most of the townspeople, so you may not see any for sale.

Romans use oil-lamps to light their homes. Lamps are made in Italy, Gaul (France) or Africa and exported to the rest of the empire.

The Romans are famous for their wine. You may have seen amphorae like these at home, because wine is exported in them to all parts of the empire.

A ship is loaded at the quay. The two oars at the stern are for steering.

The beautiful glossy red Samian ware pottery comes from Gaul. It is so popular it is an important export item.

Wild animals are imported to fight in the town's arena. When the Colosseum in Rome opened, 5,000 animals – lions, bears, and crocodiles – were slaughtered.

Spain, Britain, and Dacia (Romania) are famous for their metals: gold, silver, and lead, while much of Rome's grain comes from North Africa.

TIME-TRAVELER'S GUIDE

CLIMATE & CLOTHES

This Roman town has a pleasant climate, with an average temperature of around 77°F (25°C) in July and August and around 46°F (8°C) in January. Most of the rain falls in late fall and winter. Summer is usually quite dry, apart from some thunderstorms.

Although some men still wear togas on very formal occasions, a knee-length tunic of linen in summer and fine wool in winter is far more popular these days. Women wear the fashionable ankle-length stola and, out of doors, they often add a long scarf or veil to protect their hairstyles. Comfortable leather sandals are the best footwear, especially if you are going to do a lot of sightseeing. For winter evenings men and boys will probably need a cloak and women and girls a palla (shawl).

Very young boys and girls will be most comfortable in short tunics, belted at the waist. As they reach their teens, however, girls will probably prefer to wear a stola and boys a toga for special occasions.

EATING OUT

You'll have so many choices when looking for somewhere to eat! So few of the smaller houses and apartments have cooking facilities that most people eat out every day. Some of the best eating-places are around the forum, but there are inns and snack-bars all over the town. Paintings on the walls act as a menu. Dishes are usually simple things such as eggs, cheese, lentils, or watermelon. Around the market and the shops you'll also find people selling ready-cooked sausages and cooked chicken pieces in the street.

If you don't like the local wine don't worry, there is a choice of non-alcoholic drinks. Grape juice is always good and honeywater can be refreshing on a hot day.

If you are lucky enough to have an introduction to one of the town's wealthy families, you may be invited to a dinner party. You could be served parrot cooked with dates, or sows' udders stuffed with sea urchins.

TOILETS & HYGIENE

As in all Roman towns, there are plenty of public toilets. The easiest to find are those in the forum, but there are others near the shops, the theater, at the public baths, and in residential areas. The public baths (see pages 30-31) are open to visitors as well as townspeople. There are separate bathing facilities for men and women, so you can go whenever you want. But remember, if you go on to visit a smaller town, the baths are also likely to be smaller, so men and women use them on different days or at different times of the day. It's best to check before you go.

Because this is quite a large town, you will find a barber and a hairdresser at the baths as well as someone who will remove unwanted hair from your arms and legs with tweezers and special creams. If this beautician is not very skilful the treatment can be quite painful, but most Romans are prepared to put up with this because it is fashionable to have smooth skin.

TIME-TRAVELER'S GUIDE

WHERE TO STAY

Although there are several inns where you can stay in the town, none of them is really suitable for tourists. Instead, they cater to people such as soldiers on leave or sailors spending a few days in port waiting for another ship. As a result they only provide basic facilities, they tend to be noisy and are frequently dirty. It may come as a surprise, because the Romans seem so well organized, but these inns are not regulated in any way. This means that the best places for tourists to stay is with family or friends in the town.

If you do not know anyone here, however, it might be possible to arrange to rent a house for a short while. This is especially true in the summer when some of the wealthy merchants move out to their villas in the country or on the coast and so would be glad to have someone living in their town houses to discourage thieves and robbers. If you decide to do this, be sure to find out in advance if they are leaving any of their servants behind to look after you, otherwise you will need to bring your own.

ETIQUETTE

Many of the rules of etiquette concern eating and drinking. It is quite acceptable to eat in the street, although snack-bars and inns usually have somewhere you can sit down. If you have a meal in a private house, you will be expected to recline on a low couch to eat. And don't forget to take your own napkin with you. There will be no forks, so you will eat with your fingers. In between courses a slave will bring you a bowl of water in which you can wash your hands. The meal will probably be huge, but don't worry if you start to feel too full when you're only part way through, no one will mind if you go to the vomitorium to be sick and then come back and start eating again. You'll find that everyone else does the same.

No matter how hard you try, you'll probably not be able to eat all the food offered to you, as there will be far too much – as custom demands. You'll find your napkin comes in useful to wrap up some of the leftovers to take home to eat next day. And, before thanking your host, do remember to wash your hands.

PERSONAL SECURITY

As in all towns, there is a danger that you will have your money stolen in a crowded area such as the market or shopping streets. For this reason, try to get a wrist purse of the sort that soldiers often wear because these can only be opened when they are removed from the wrist. Hiring an attendant to look after your belongings if you go to the public baths is also a good idea. Apart from a few pickpockets, however, the streets are quite safe during the day, but do remember to watch out for the traffic which is quite heavy in some streets, especially around the market and docks.

At night you are safe, too, so long as you use your common sense and don't go wandering alone after dark as the streets are unlit and you could easily get lost, be attacked, or have an accident.

You must also be careful about approaching any house with a sign saying CAVE CANEM. This means you must beware of the dog and, as the townspeople give their dogs names such as "Ferox" (fierce) or "Celer" (swift), it is wise to take the warning seriously!

TIME-TRAVELER'S GUIDE

MEDICAL TREATMENT

If you become ill or have an accident while visiting the town, there are a number of good doctors who will treat you. If you can afford it, they will come and visit you, but otherwise you will have to go to them. If you are seriously ill and know the right people, such as a high-ranking official or army officer, you could take advantage of the health care provided by the government for such people.

The best doctors are those who did their training in Greece or in the army. Army-trained doctors are quite good at setting broken bones. After all, a lame soldier, or one who cannot use his sword arm, is of no use to the Roman army!

If it is just a minor health problem that is bothering you, go to a pharmacist who will sell you a remedy made from herbs, other plants, and minerals. You can also try spending the night in the shrine of Aesculapius, the god of medicine, in the hope of having a dream that will show you how to cure your illness.

MONEY, WEIGHTS, & MEASURES

You'll find understanding Roman money and weights and measures quite easy because they are more or less the same wherever you are in the empire.

The currency is based on gold and silver coins, although you are unlikely to see any gold ones, which are usually issued just to the troops on special occasions, for example when a new emperor comes to power.

Most coins in everyday use are silver or bronze. There are 25 silver denarii to each gold aureus. You may come across other bronze coins because different areas within the empire also issue their own coins. Try to avoid these coins because shopkeepers and stall-holders may not accept them.

Weights and measures are based on the Roman pound or libra (about a quarter of a pound). They are standard all over the empire and officials make regular checks at the markets to ensure that no one is being cheated.

LANGUAGE

You'll hear many different languages in the streets of the town, as merchants and visitors from other parts of the empire crowd its streets and markets. The official language is Latin, the language that was spoken by the original inhabitants of Rome, and most people can at least understand the basics of it. If you really don't know any Latin, you should, as a matter of good manners, learn to say *Salve* (Hello) and *Vale* (Goodbye).

The Latin alphabet has 22 letters and when it is written down it can be a little confusing because a capital I is used for both I and J and a capital V is used for both V and U. This means that JULIUS is written as IVLIVS and JULIA is written as IVLIA.

You'll notice that capital letters are used for inscriptions on buildings, tombstones, and memorials. When people want to write notes or letters to each other, however, they use a flowing, rounded script which is easier to write, but is not always easy to read.

TIME-TRAVELER'S GUIDE

ENTERTAINMENT & SPORTS FACILITIES

You'll find plenty of entertainment to choose from. As well as the theater (described on pages 16 and 17) and the amphitheater (pages 18 and 19), there is also the circus where chariot races are held. These are very exciting and might suit you if you do not want to watch people killing each other. In the streets you can watch jugglers and acrobats or listen to musicians playing instruments such as the pan-pipes and the lyre.

If you're feeling more serious, you can go to the forum and listen to a politician making a speech to persuade people to vote for him. And don't forget the town's excellent library, where you can read a wide range of scrolls or attend a public reading of the latest work by a well-known author.

Enjoyed the local food and wine too much? Never mind, the public baths (pages 30 and 31) have the best sports facilities and you can get back in shape with weight-lifting or gymnastics in the exercise yard.

SHOPPING

The best shops in town are those around the forum and in the streets where the wealthy merchants live – you can tell which these streets are very easily by the size of the houses. In the shops in these areas you can buy high-quality jewelery, pottery, glassware, and silverware. You can also buy wigs and hairpieces for men and women, as well as makeup for the eyes and powders to make your skin fashionably pale. As you would expect in an area like this, these shops are expensive, so, unless you are very rich, just go and look at the goods they have on offer.

For serious shopping, go to the shops in the less wealthy parts of the town, like those on pages 32 and 33, where you can often see the craftsmen making the goods they sell in the shops. They will usually make things to order at little extra cost. Don't forget that shops generally close in the hottest part of the day – but it is not much fun shopping in the heat anyway.

TOYS & GAMES

This town is a good place in which to buy toys and games for your children, or any nieces and nephews you may have. Especially popular are wooden dolls with movable joints, but there are also rag dolls and dolls modeled from clay and painted. Kites, hoops, whips, and tops and balls are also in demand.

For the very young there are carved wooden animals on wheels which can be pulled along. There are also toy mice, birds and dogs which are modelled in clay or cast in bronze and are just the right size for a small child to hold.

You'll be able to buy dice, counters and boards for games, such as checkers as well as knucklebones, or tali, which are numbered on the sides and thrown like dice.

Do you have any geese at home? If you do, what about buying a two-wheeled cart that can be pulled by a pair of them? The carts may be common here, but you'll be popular with your children because none of their friends will have one.

RELIGION

There are many different temples and shrines in the town (pages 28 and 29) and each one has its own gods and goddesses and its own priests and priestesses. They will make sacrifices and offer prayers on your behalf if you want them to, but you must also remember to offer a prayer every day to the lares, the gods of the house in which you are staying. This is to ensure that the household will be protected from such misfortunes as fire, robbery, hunger, and bad luck. It is also said to help if you leave small gifts of food for the lares. They are especially fond of fruit, cheese, and honey cakes.

Astrologers and fortune-tellers will tell you your future, for a price, but the practice is frowned upon and few sophisticated Romans do this.

LOCAL CUSTOMS & FESTIVALS

There are many different festivals and celebrations in the town each year. Most of them were originally held for religious reasons, but now they are often just an excuse for a public holiday with games and races, picnics, feasting, and drinking. One which is just a family occasion is Parentalia which takes place between February 13th and 21st. At this time people visit the cemeteries outside the town (pages 14 and 15) and take milk, wine, and flowers for their dead parents. This will stop them coming back to haunt the living. On March 14th horse races are held in the circus to mark the feast of Mars and between April 12th and April 19th there are games in honor of the goddess Ceres who makes the harvest grow. Between April 28th and May 3rd there is a carnival dedicated to Flora, goddess of flowers. A feast is held to honor Mercury on August 12th. However, the biggest and most popular feast of all begins on December 17th and is called Saturnalia, after the god Saturn. It lasts for up to seven days and there are games and a great deal of feasting. There is also a special ceremony in which masters wait on their slaves for a day.

GETTING AROUND THE TOWN

If you are really wealthy, you might like to do your sight-seeing the lazy way – by being taken around the streets and sights in a sedan chair or bed, carried on the shoulders of slaves. You will be able to lie back against soft pillows and be shaded from the heat of the sun by a canopy. This is not really as comfortable an option as it may

sound at first, because the bed can sway a good deal and so could make you feel sick. (If this does happen, chewing on a fresh mint leaf is a good remedy.)

For most people, however, walking is the best way to get around the town, as most of the important places are quite close together. Because the streets are paved all you really need is a pair of comfortable sandals. But do take care when you are crossing the road as the wheels of passing carts have worn two deep grooves in all the main streets and it is very easy to trip on them. Another hazard is water, which always collects in the streets and wheel grooves after heavy rain. You can use the rows of stepping stones to cross the streets to avoid getting your feet wet, but look out that your clothes don't get splashed and spoilt by passing carts.

If the worst does happen, and your clothes do get drenched in filthy water, you will need to have them cleaned. There are two or three fullers in town who will do this for you. Send a servant with the dirty clothes to the fuller's shop and he will first bleach them by spreading them out on wooden frames under which a pot of sulphur is burning. Then the clothes are washed in a large tub of water and fuller's earth, which is a type of clay. The fuller, or his assistant, treads all over the clothes to get the dirt out. After that they are dried in the sun and pressed. Then they are ready for your servant to collect for you.

TRAVELING OUTSIDE THE TOWN

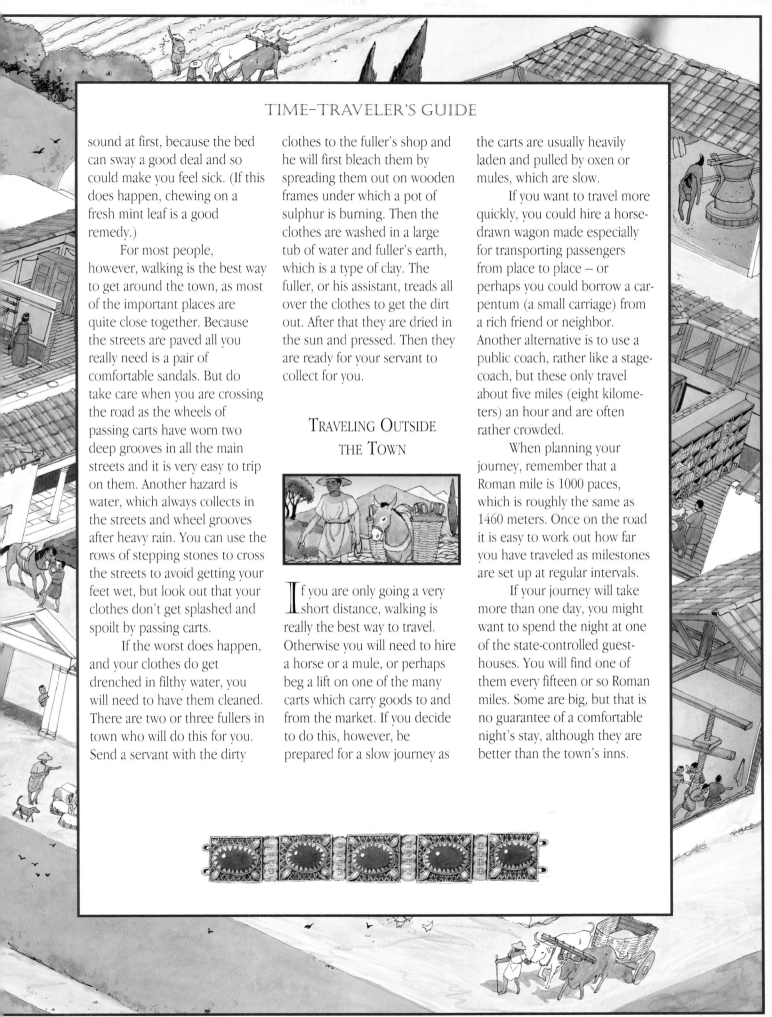

If you are only going a very short distance, walking is really the best way to travel. Otherwise you will need to hire a horse or a mule, or perhaps beg a lift on one of the many carts which carry goods to and from the market. If you decide to do this, however, be prepared for a slow journey as the carts are usually heavily laden and pulled by oxen or mules, which are slow.

If you want to travel more quickly, you could hire a horse-drawn wagon made especially for transporting passengers from place to place – or perhaps you could borrow a car-pentum (a small carriage) from a rich friend or neighbor. Another alternative is to use a public coach, rather like a stage-coach, but these only travel about five miles (eight kilometers) an hour and are often rather crowded.

When planning your journey, remember that a Roman mile is 1000 paces, which is roughly the same as 1460 meters. Once on the road it is easy to work out how far you have traveled as milestones are set up at regular intervals.

If your journey will take more than one day, you might want to spend the night at one of the state-controlled guest-houses. You will find one of them every fifteen or so Roman miles. Some are big, but that is no guarantee of a comfortable night's stay, although they are better than the town's inns.

GUIDED TOURS

THE TOWN CENTER

The best place to start your tour is at the forum (you'll find it described on pages 20 and 21), as that is easy to reach from all parts of the town. Do a little window-shopping and dream of all the things you would buy if you suddenly inherited a fortune, then come back to earth and look on any of the market stalls for some fine fresh fruit and vegetables. Depending on the season, cabbages, and leeks are a popular choice, especially if you can get fresh coriander to flavor them with. And, if you're feeling hungry already, try some stuffed dates from Marcus's stall near the fountain. They are on the expensive side, but quite definitely the best you'll ever taste!

Opposite the fountain you'll find the shrine of Ceres, the goddess of the harvest. Then, if you turn to your right, you'll be facing the basilica. If you have time, go inside and visit one of the law courts. If you are lucky there might be an interesting trial taking place, but don't stay too long as there is still plenty to see in the town.

Leave the forum by any of the exits leading on to the Via Principalis (the main street) and cross the road to visit the temple (pages 28 and 29). You can admire the fine carvings on the front of the temple and see the altar on which sacrifices are made to give thanks to the gods or to ask them for favors.

A short street up the side of the temple leads to the public baths (for more details see pages 30 and 31). You won't have time to use their facilities now, but it's useful to know where they are for another day.

Back on the Via Principalis, start walking towards the gate leading to the river and you will quickly come to some very interesting shops (pages 32 and 33), where you can buy your presents and souvenirs at more reasonable prices than you could in the shops around the forum. For the ladies, Caius the goldsmith does some very pretty gold ear-rings in the shape of dolphins, while for the men he stocks handsome signet rings. Titus the shoemaker sells the most comfortable sandals in town and Marius the cloth-merchant claims to have the finest linen in the empire for making tunics and stolas. You're sure to be thirsty by this time, however, so remember to save some money for a visit to the bar run by Julius and his wife Livia, and buy yourself a glass of spiced wine or honeywater.

THE TOWN CENTER
AND
THE DOCKS

Start from the forum, as in the Town Center Tour, but after visiting the shops, carry on down the Via Principalis to the gate at the end. Go through this and you will find yourself on the quayside (pages 34 and 35), overlooking the river and the bridge which crosses it. With the gate behind you, look to your left and you will see the aqueduct which brings fresh water into the town from the

distant hills. Then, nearer to the bridge, but on the opposite bank of the river, you will see the army camp (pages 26 and 27). The strong high fence will prevent you seeing much of what's happening on the parade ground inside, but you may just be lucky enough to see some of the soldiers training in the flat fields nearby.

If you like watching other people at work, go down onto the quayside and watch some of the boats being loaded and unloaded. There are plenty of quayside bars where you can linger while you're watching all the comings and goings.

When you've tired of this, go back through the gate into the Via Principalis. Walk past the first block of houses then take the next street on your left. At the end nearest the town wall you will find one of the houses of the wealthy merchants (they are described on pages 20 and 21). You won't be able to go in, of course, but if the door to the atrium is open, take a quick glance inside and see how calm and peaceful everything looks in

there compared to the noise and bustle of the streets.

A right turn at the end of the merchant's house will bring you into a street leading to the theater (see pages 16 and 17) and, as you approach, you might just see some of the actors. Even if you've already seen them on stage, you probably won't be able to recognize them as, without their wigs, masks, and platform boots, they look just like everyone else! Then, from the theater it is just a matter of crossing the road and you'll be back in the forum – and probably more than ready for something to eat.

THE TOWN
AND ITS
OUTSKIRTS

Explore the town as described in the previous tour, but, once you've seen the theater, do not cross the street back to the forum. Instead, turn to your left and after one block turn left again to leave the town by the west gate. The road you

will then find yourself on has some of the most interesting tombstones you could wish to see (pages 14 and 15). Some look like small temples, while others are carved with detailed pictures of the person buried in them and scenes from his or her life. Some of the inscriptions are very touching, too, especially the one to the devoted mother who died while trying to rescue her baby from a fire in one of the apartments.

Once past the tombstones, a short walk will bring you to a road on your left that will take you to the amphitheater (pages 18 and 19). The road will be very crowded if there is anything going on there.

A little farther on there is a turning to the right. This leads to the handsome villa in the distance surrounded by its cornfields and vineyards (you'll find more details on pages 12 and 13). Both the amphitheater and the villa are well worth visiting, but you'll almost certainly need those new sandals if you want to go to both!

GLOSSARY

Amphora (plural **amphorae**) large earthenware container used for storing liquids.

Aqueduct stone structure to carry fresh water from the hills into a town.

Atrium open courtyard in the center of a house.

Basilica large public building that served as the town hall and law courts.

Brazier metal container in which a fire could burn safely.

Caldarium the hot room at the baths with a heated pool.

Cremation burning a dead body until only ashes remained. The Romans then put the ashes in a container called an urn and buried it.

Curia the building where the town council met to discuss government affairs.

Dacia the area of eastern Europe now known as Romania.

Frigidarium the room at the baths with a large unheated swimming pool.

Hobnail nail with a thick, strong head that stood out from the sole of the sandal, to stop it wearing out too quickly.

Impluvium open courtyard where rainwater for use in the house was collected in a pool.

Laconicum the hottest room at the baths. It had a tub of boiling water in the middle to keep it hot and steamy.

Lararium shrine to the lares, the household gods, found in every Roman home.

Lares the household gods.

Liquamen popular sauce made from fermented fish. It was very strong and may have helped hide the taste of food that was not completely fresh.

Palla woolen shawl worn by Roman women in cold weather.

Peristylium private walled garden; usually only found in the homes of the wealthy.

Stola long, loose-fitting dress worn by Roman women. It could be made from linen, wool, cotton, or silk.

Strigil flat-bladed scraper used to remove the mixture of dirt, sweat, and oil from the body at the baths.

Stylus pointed metal implement used for writing on wax tablets.

Tablinium room used as a study in a private house.

Tabularium building where the town's records were kept.

Tepidarium the warm room at the baths which had a small pool.

Toga garment worn by men and boys. Made from a semi-circular piece of cloth, three times as long as a man was tall, it was worn draped over the left shoulder, across the back, under the right arm, across the chest, and then back over the left shoulder.

Triclinium the dining-room of a house.

Underworld (also known as Hades), this was where a dead person's spirit was thought to go to be judged, before going on to Elysium (heaven) or Tartarus (hell).

INDEX

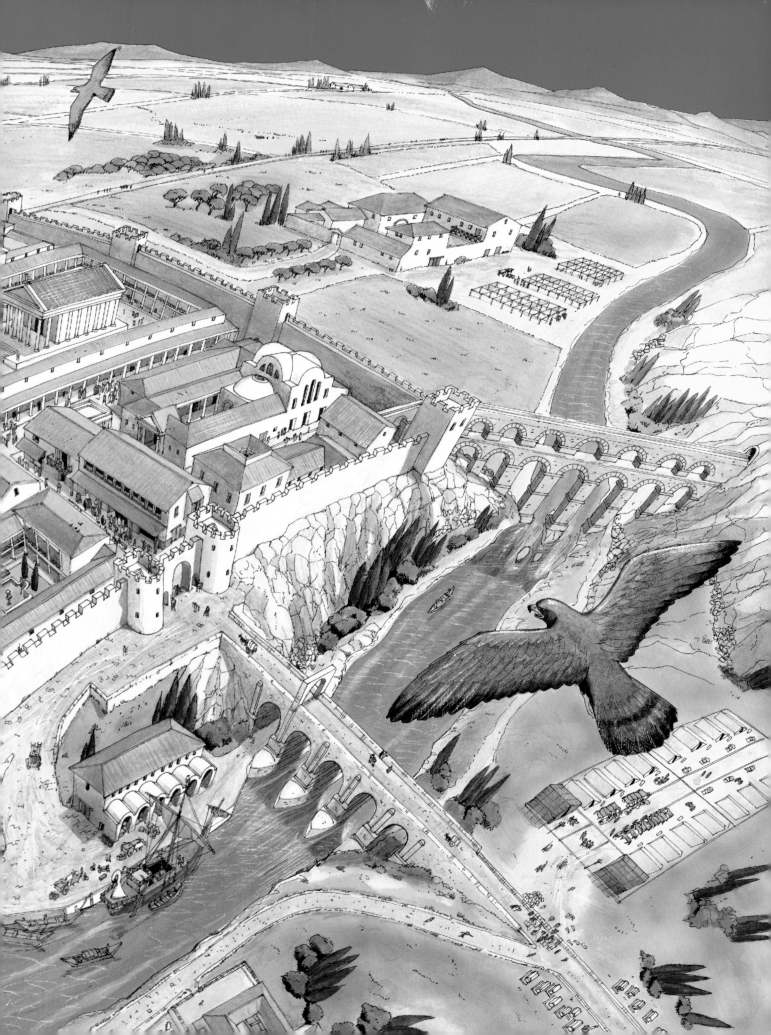